JOURNEY INTO GROWTH

JOURNEY INTO GROWTH

The Seven Core Values of a Mission Church

CENTRE FOR MISSION ACCOMPANIMENT

Edited by Terry Tennens

Churches Together in Britain and Ireland

Contents

The Accompanied Mission Journey

Appendix

Further resources and contact information

Foreword

How can church life grow in mission? This question is central to many discussions in and about churches today. At national, local or regional level the concerns are similar. In a world where institutions are declining can churches buck the trend and how will that be achieved?

For over ten years *Building Bridges of Hope* has observed a representative sample of churches in England, Wales, Scotland and Ireland with a key question at the heart of their enquiries: 'What ways of being church enable local Christian communities to join effectively in the mission of God?'

The Seven Core Values of a Mission Church are the distillation of that research and are offered here to churches as resources for their growth and development. They are relevant for small and larger churches, rural, urban and suburban, since the original research included representative churches from many different contexts in England, Scotland, Wales and Ireland.

One core value, however, stood out above all others in the journey of growth: an openness to receive the insights of the skilled outsider. Popularly known as mission accompaniment, this openness was evident in all growing church communities. *Journey into Growth* brings together the process of mission accompaniment and the core values of a mission church.

The intention behind *Journey into Growth* is that it will encourage churches to look at themselves and seek the companionship of the skilled outsider – the mission companion – in working through *Journey into Growth* as church communities.

I warmly commend *Journey into Growth* to all churches who want to grow in mission.

Janice Price
Executive Secretary
Global Mission Network
of Churches Together in Britain and Ireland
www.missionaccompaniment.com

Acknowledgements

We would like to express thanks and appreciation to the churches and mission companions whom we learnt from during the Building Bridges of Hope project. To the Executive staff who initiated, ignited and supported Building Bridges of Hope, special thanks being due to Donald Elliott, Simon Barrow and Janice Price. For the seconded and volunteer Development Group members in England, Wales, Scotland and Ireland – you have been inspirational!

Thanks are also due to David Banks of bankcartoons for the cartoons which illustrate the text so vividly.

Finally, to the CMA writing group: Andrew Brookes, John Cole, Teresa Kirk, Eilis O'Malley and Philip Walker – my personal thanks for sustaining me for the journey into growth.

Terry R. Tennens
Editor

Introduction

How to make the best use of this material

There are a variety of methods that could be used to benefit from *Journey into Growth*. There is not a 'one size fits all' approach. It depends whether you are addressing the themes of the seven core values for the first time, or whether you have addressed these in recent years and the purpose is to reinvigorate the mission plan.

Journey into Growth could be used by a PCC, pastoral teams, Elders or Deacons' groups by having a series of away days or evenings, separate from the business meetings already held, to give space to grasp afresh the sense of purpose and direction. Even if you have a clear vision or mission statement, you could consider more deeply how is it being lived out?

At the same time *Journey into Growth* could be used in a preaching plan linked to mid-week home or cell groups addressing the seven core values Bible studies. The benefit of the Sunday preaching plan is that it includes those who do not participate in a mid-week home group.

Following the series, the leadership of the church could invite some speakers to contribute their experience on a given core value. Or after the conclusion to the series you could plan two or three mid-week gatherings to hear together some of the findings from other home groups and to see what pattern for future possibilities is taking shape.

Following the study it would be wise, if one is not already in position, to appoint a mission companion to assist the church in avoiding loss of momentum. The church could also draw up an agreed programme, using church and community audits, and even appoint a co-ordination group overseeing the *Journey into Growth* process with the mission companion.

The important principles are that everyone is invited into the process of listening and sharing; that the process is open and, given busy occasions during the church year with feasts and festivals, a sensible time-line is established to achieve milestones.

So set a pace that keeps a rhythm and is realistic. Be accountable to one another by being transparent, honest, constructive and discerning. Link all that's happening to the prayer life of the church. Keep communicating using Sunday prayers, newsletters and gatherings to keep people informed and motivated to see fruit from *Journey into Growth*.

A Brief Overview of Mission Accompaniment

The purpose of this short section is to give an overview of mission accompaniment and the people who carry it out and the skills this involves. After looking in some detail at the values of a mission church – factors proposed here as useful ways of identifying needs for accompaniment and specific ways of then structuring such a process – we shall return to the subject of mission accompaniment and its practical implementation in more detail. However, it is helpful to have and retain an overview of what is involved from the outset.

What is mission accompaniment?

Mission accompaniment is the term that is increasingly being used to describe a process undertaken by a local church (inherited or emerging) in conjunction with an outsider to help them develop as mission communities. This person – this outsider who comes alongside – is described in various ways. In this handbook, the term 'mission companion' has been used. However, other terms are used by other churches and agencies that have done developmental work in this area. These include mission accompanier, enabler, facilitator, mission coach, encourager, adviser. Others could be added. However, there is increasing agreement of the broad nature of the role and the core skills that exercising it involves.

Thus, there are a number of ways to understand the role of the mission companion, for instance:

the friendly stranger using the Emmaus Road story;

the skilful outsider who uses their talent as facilitator;

enablers who release the potential in people;

advisers who signpost a range of resources out there.

Indeed, it is thus being recognised that these are different ways of describing the same, or similar, process and person who carries it out.

Mission companions are fellow Christians whose attitude and demeanour is to serve the Lord's people and his Church. They are not there to tell you what to do, rather, assist you in discovering afresh God's will that is unique to your church or project and context. Therefore, servanthood is a key quality in the sense of being one who journeys alongside others.

The primary skills of mission companions

Mission companions need to develop and use a number of skills to be effective. These include:

- Listening
- Questioning
- Discussing
- Reflecting
- Interpreting
- Facilitating
- Signposting

Examples of how these are used will be found throughout this handbook.

The methodology of mission accompaniment

Mission accompaniment can have a loose agenda and a very fluid structure, or both of these can be more defined and structured. If structuring is used, this is not to reduce flexibility and life but rather to allow energy and, hopefully, grace to flow better and be more fruitful.

Mission accompaniment, as developed here, has a method that uses the 'seven core values of a mission church'. These are:

1. Focusing vision
2. Building local partnerships
3. Sharing faith and values
4. Nourishing daily living
5. Developing shared leadership
6. Becoming communities of learning
7. Contributing to and participating in wider networks

These provide the lens through which the mission companion helps the church to look at itself. Each local congregation is unique, therefore, one size does not fit all and that is why mission accompaniment is customised in each specific use. In each church or project to be accompanied, a specific selection of these values is made and then also the content of these is honed to suit the exact situation of the church-mission project. Once agreed on, these then provide the agenda or framework by which the mission companion and the church journey forward together into growth and a deeper participation in mission.

Biblical foundations for mission accompaniment

The term 'mission accompaniment' is a recent one but an examination of the Bible shows that its cores skills and attitudes were practised there. Often we read of someone coming alongside another person and journeying with them and, as they do that, listening, sharing ideas, making suggestions, casting light on a situation, encouraging, even challenging sensitively. In doing this, they allow mission to go forward and God's plans to be more fully realised. All of this means growth of God's kingdom. Examples include Jethro with Moses (Exodus 18), Barnabas with Paul (Acts 11-15) and then Paul in his turn with other co-workers. It is also clear that Jesus did this too. He practised many of these accompaniment skills in training his disciples. The way Jesus journeyed with the disciples on the road to Emmaus, bringing them to renewed and deeper faith to such a degree that they went out in mission carrying the resurrection news to the other disciples (Luke 24.13-35) is perhaps the clearest model for mission accompaniment.[1] The companion does not take over but helps the other person achieve the mission that God is calling them to.

In a way we can say that this touches on something very central to all of Salvation History. God comes alongside his people – collectively or through specific individuals – journeying with them, helping them fulfil the purpose and mission he has already given them but doing this in a way that respects their autonomy, freedom and character. God and his initiative are central to all this. God goes ahead of us in mission (the Missio Dei) but also comes alongside us, indicating to us how we can be instruments in his mission.

This takes us to the Divine heart of accompaniment. The Greek word, usually rendered as 'paraclete' means in English literally 'the one who comes alongside'. Jesus and then especially the Holy Spirit are described by this term (John 14 and 16). Obviously, the Holy Spirit works through human agents – but that is all we are asked to be – his instruments. Thus, it is the Spirit of Jesus who hopefully animates the process of mission accompaniment, bringing his grace, light, discernment,

---

1. For more on these and other Scripture passages and how to apply them practically to mission accompaniment see Philip Walker Mission Accompaniment, Grove, 2005, pp. 13-16.

prophetic insight, knowledge, wisdom and love so that all move forward in grace and fruitfulness. Mission companions, and those being accompanied, use all their human skills and training, but especially look to God in prayer.

Through this, God's people are called to journey into growth, that is, growth in more effective service and participation in mission and, with that, growth into holiness and wholeness and a fullness of blessing and life in Christ. God is the way and the means as well as the end of the journey.

The Seven Core Values of a Mission Church

The seven core values of a mission church are features of local churches, emerging churches and other mission projects that have repeatedly been recognised as being important to their life, health and especially their missionary vigour and fruitfulness. Reflection on them is likely to be helpful whether or not mission accompaniment is finally adopted and, if so, how this is practised.

1. Focusing vision – discovering God's pathway

Introduction

Why are we here? How shall we live together? Where is God leading us?

These are the primary questions that emerge from this first core value on 'focusing vision'.

Purpose, values and vision are incredibly important to your local church especially in changing times. This is not a management exercise of drawing up purpose statements that are simply great ideas. What can then often happen is that they lie dormant on the notice board, rarely mentioned ever again.

Focusing vision is a spiritual exercise of discerning how God wants to lead your Christian community. It's discovering and naming what makes your church heartbeat tick. Where do your concerns, passion and convictions lie?

You as a church are a unique Christian community, in that you are placed in a specific context, with a particular history, with a unique gathering of believers, called, gifted and prepared for service. No local church looks the same. We see this in the New Testament with the Jerusalem church and the Corinthian church that were so different, yet bound as one under the headship of Christ.

Now your clarity of purpose, for example, could be, 'to Love God and love our neighbours'. This is unlikely to change significantly for ten or thirty years.

The values of your community also will remain clear, such as welcoming the stranger and being a community that practises forgiveness and reconciliation.

However, your vision or mission statement is usually short to medium term – two to seven years. The vision is profoundly influenced by your purpose and your values. Therefore, if your purpose is to share the love of Christ in witness and service in the wider community and your values are about integrity, honesty, love and welcome, it's incompatible to express your vision exclusively on internal church life, such as amazing small groups, when your purpose is about reaching out as well as in.

The story – Tallaght Methodist Church, Dublin

Here is a vision and values statement of a relatively new Christian community with a purpose-built church and community centre in a sprawling urban setting that was challenged by multiple social and deprivation indicators.

The church established the following three-year vision:

- To create an innovative and varied programme in the church centre and in people's homes which meets the spiritual, emotional and physical needs of people.
- To attract people into the worshipping community and into partnership in the work of mission.
- To build a dynamic team of workers, professional and lay, drawn from both inside and outside the community in Tallaght.
- To become more financially independent.
- The church service to move to the main hall, every room in the centre being used, and a big bus in the car park for transporting people to the centre.
- A band to lead worship.
- Drop-in centre for lonely people.
- Preachers from within the congregation.
- To be a church known in the area as a loving community, a people of faith and where everyone receives a warm welcome.

A new church with a new vision sustaining them for three years is now becoming a reality. They moved from a gathering of individuals into a focused and vision-driven group.

How was this achieved?

1. They articulated and discerned God's mission and vision.
2. They received the support of a skilful outsider (mission accompanier).
3. They are now implementing the vision into action plans.

Application

Tallaght Methodist Church has become a purposeful Christian community with a new community centre, a place and a people with a warm welcome, used by various groups to sustain their spirituality, daily lives, youth groups and young parents. They are living the life and sharing the story of Christ, as a multi-functional church from a small group of people, yet galvanised through determined steps, with support from their denomination and beyond.

What is your church's vision?

Matthew 17.17-21 (The Message)

Jesus said, 'What a generation! No sense of God! No focus to your lives! How many times do I have to go over these things? How much longer do I have to put up with this? Bring the boy here.' He ordered the afflicting demon out – and it was out, gone. From that moment on the boy was well. When the disciples had Jesus all to themselves, they asked, 'Why couldn't we throw it out?'

'Because you're not yet taking God seriously,' said Jesus. 'The simple truth is that if you had a mere kernel of faith, a poppy seed, say, you would tell this mountain, "Move!" and it would move. There is nothing you wouldn't be able to tackle.'

Suggested activities

- Put aside the real and imagined reasons why the mountains in your church context are too big to handle. Spend a moment freely and creatively imagining how the Lord desires your church to be fearless, involved in serving the community, partnering other groups and sharing faith. Spend some moments sharing these together uncritically.

- Consider doing a listening survey within the congregation, to the communities surrounding the church and other organisations, such as parish council or local schools and voluntary groups. Identify the nature of the needs they specify and how they perceive the value of your church. From this conduct further enquiries to see whether the church could serve in collaborative ways.

Questions

- Does the story of Tallaght Methodist Church connect with you? Describe how?
- Where do you need to grow faith in your church?
- What mountains around you are metaphors of fear and lead to paralysis of action?
- How will Tallaght's story and the scripture passage help you discover the little and often unseen gifts that can germinate into the kingdom of God?

- Do you have a focus for your community life? What is it? How do you put this into practice? Do you all agree on the vision?

- What for you is a compelling goal? It could be a mixture of 'I belong to this church because of its purpose – define your church's purpose.' It could be the values in community life together – define the values intrinsic in your church community. It may be direction where the church is heading, the mission and vision – what enthuses you about your church's direction?

- Finally, if you are still stuck with the language of this vision approach – let's try looking at it in a different way, in reverse.

    (a) What would it be like if your church did not exist?

    (b) What would be missing? Are there any gains if the church were not present?

    (c) What would a local church look like that was only serving the needs of members and not people in the wider community?

    (d) Is God pleased with how your church is living the life and sharing the story of Christ? If so, how? If not, why not?

Your situation will not be exactly like this story – it is not your story, but what can you learn from it?

2. Building local partnerships – community engagement

Introduction

A bridge is a structure to connect two ends that would otherwise be disconnected. In the Gospel of John chapter 1 verse 14, which says 'the word became a human being', there is a sense that Jesus is the bridge between heaven and earth, the creator and the created, uniting both sides. Continuing in the theme of John's Gospel, one of the great thrusts in Christian mission is that of reconciliation, the bringing together, often of unlikely partners, in pursuit of wholeness and hope.

The cross as a symbol of the Christian faith continues the metaphor with the crossbeam intersecting the vertical bar. The former reflects on the bridge across humanity and the latter the bridge between God and humanity and the whole cosmos.

Consequently, your local church is a bridging station, a community that represents God's presence and another way of seeing life. Therefore, God's mission beckons us to embrace the world for the love of Christ. This is enormously challenging, since it leads to the notion of emptying ourselves (Philippians 2.1-7) in the service of God. However, it can be very rewarding to see the influence Christians can have as salt and light. We know this is true in Christian history through the abolition of slavery, the provision of education for children, welfare and health provision – the successes of Christians who have partnered one another as reformers.

Building local partnerships as a core value is understood not simply as building inter-church relationships – as valuable as that is in the pursuit of the mission of God – but also as considering what non-church agencies (voluntary, statutory, government and private sector) our churches can partner for mutual aims.

However altruistic church life can be, we need to be clear about what is and what is not achievable, and must not over-extend ourselves with too many partnerships. Also we need to take care that our Christian distinctiveness is not lost because our faith and values become indistinct. However, the benefits of integrating both the secular and spiritual life are significant.

The story – Frontline Centre, Liverpool

This thriving city-centre, independent cell church with over 700 adherents purchased a redundant Royal Mail sorting office to facilitate the bridge-building mission they were called to.

As a Christian community they have a thriving children's and youth ministry. They transport young people across the city. They regularly visit the homes from which the children come.

The church works with refugees, has spearheaded the work of the SureStart initiative and chairs the Liverpool Faith Network.

Here are the values of the Liverpool Faith Network:

1. To work in unity, celebrate diversity and to bring spiritual values to the heart of policy;
2. To constantly strive for social justice, human rights and equity in all areas of the work;
3. To be inclusive and extend membership to the diverse range of grass roots organisations that meet membership criteria and promote goodwill and fellowship between faith communities;
4. To increase involvement from the faith communities in the city's Local Strategic Partnership and to contribute to decision making on the better delivery of public services, policy and issues of concern to faith communities;
5. To bring together community and voluntary-sector views in the area of faith(s), to identify key issues and help develop solutions;
6. To elect representatives to take part in the Local Strategic Partnership or its sub-groups as well as to assist in consultation, planning and commissioning forums;
7. To use the network structure as a means of presenting a broad range of opinions, knowledge and insights from the city's community voluntary and faith sectors.

Application – Priority Areas Committee, Church of Scotland

The challenge in any bridge-building is when it involves partners of inequality. In Glasgow, the Priority Areas Committee has engaged in this by allowing the less powerful partner to determine the methods of engagement and reporting into what are often middle-class, affluent structures in our churches. Therefore, the cautionary note is that the more powerful partners need to act with gentleness and respect in order to permit the disempowered partner to determine the motivation of interest to serve.

John 4.6-9 (NIV)

Jesus tired as he was from the journey, sat down by the well. It was about the sixth hour. When a Samaritan woman came to draw water, Jesus said to her, 'Will you give me a drink?' (His disciples had gone into town to buy food.) The Samaritan woman said to him, 'You are a Jew and I am a Samaritan woman. How can you ask me for a drink?' (For Jews do not associate with Samaritans.)

Suggested activities

- Now that you have examined what is already in existence, brainstorm the real needs in your community. Use the values of the Liverpool Faith Network as a starting point, but remember you are discussing your area and your church and not Liverpool!

- Having a list of likely and real local needs is important, but it is unlikely that your local statutory authorities will totally agree with you, so find out what they think. Talk to Social Services, the Local Strategic Partnership, and any other group you discover in your locality. Government policy is to work with faith groups and you will need to show long-term commitment if you are to make a difference.

Questions

- What other Christian churches are you partnering? How are these being developed as partnerships for action and mission? For example, how are church buildings used for collaborative ministry to the young and elderly?

- What expertise exists within your church? What does your church excel at?

- What links do you have among voluntary groups, parish councils, schools, and social service providers? What opportunities are present for partnership?

- What links do you have with parachurch organisations to help with your local partnerships? If there are none, get someone to research the possibilities on the Internet. You may find it useful to start with Faithworks at http://www.faithworks.info/, but this is just a start.

- In the Bible passage above we find Jesus crossing barriers in the heat of the day. The Samaritan woman deliberately visited the well at the hottest time of day to avoid others. Who are the most unlikely partners in your community and why?

- How much corporate and individual prayer is being undertaken for the bridge building? Find out and then seek to increase it, especially as you discover the needs in *your* local community. In your group, remember to pray about these issues together regularly as well as individually.

- The best work is often done by committed individuals. How can you support, release and empower individuals for partnerships of impact? Kerry

Thorpe, who was Team Leader of Harvest New Anglican Church in Thanet, is the chair of the Local Strategic Partnership, and works across church streams. Do you have anyone working like this already? Can you encourage some to get involved? One possibility at this stage in your development may be as a school governor.

In the coming week please prepare for next week's study group in order to get the most from it.

3. Sharing faith and values – what, where, and how?

Introduction

Sharing faith and values as a core value indicates the importance of conversation with people beyond church circles, seeking out shared values and yearnings.

We use this expression, 'sharing faith and values', instead of the term 'evangelism' because the former is committed to a dialogue of learning, while the latter, in common understanding, though often not true to reality, can be limited to a monologue of information. Therefore, sharing faith and values means commitment to Christian integrity and being clear about our Christian roots. However, this is always coupled with the determination to respect the other in the conversation. The experience of many churches is that they have high expectations of faith sharing, but in reality it is sporadic, unconnected to community involvement and is not a priority.

In some churches small groups are an ideal avenue for Christians to learn to share their faith together. It is both affirming to be heard as well as a useful testing ground of what one does or does not say to describe one's spiritual journey in conversation with those beyond church circles.

How does what happens on a Sunday equip and empower Christians to be supported in their daily encounters to share faith and values at work, in the neighbourhood and at leisure?

Imagine if the Sunday service themes were shaped by those who face these daily encounters. Some churches allow a few minutes during worship where people describe their workplace lives so that others can understand, support, learn and pray for them.

The story – Bradford Churches Inner Ring Group

In Britain we live with three broad groups that might appear ready for evangelising. The first are those who have been Christians or who have been brought up as Christians but who no longer practise – the de-churched. The second group consists of those local people who have no church connection and are effectively un-churched. The third group includes those members of other faiths, practising and non-practising.

For many reasons, direct evangelism of those of other faiths, is usually counter-productive; and the most powerful reason is a combination of resentment and the barriers it creates in poor, tight-knit and beleaguered communities. We should instead seek to explore together and understand one another better and this includes sharing what Christian faith is and means to us, as well as understanding and hearing those who belong to other faiths. We might look for areas of shared values with those of other faiths, for example, devotion to God in prayer, learning the Scriptures and community fellowship, family and wider moral values. The Bradford Churches Inner Ring Group has been working in such a context. They include a commitment to evangelism and inter-faith dialogue, friendship and understanding in their work.

For the de-churched it is worth discovering the reasons why lapsed Christians cease to practise and we may have to re-think elements in Church behaviour that have alienated the de-churched.

Similarly, with the un-churched we need to reflect on faith and culture, and learn new ways of engaging people with the Christ story, at different times, places and with a variety of media, yet underpinned by an open community. We face the challenge of entering into a conversation with working class people who are largely excluded from middle class British churches. What does spiritual hope mean for people without hope?

Application – Harvest New Anglican Church, Broadstairs

A new Anglican cell church in Kent, 'Harvest', has five central values:
1. Jesus at the centre
2. Everybody growing
3. Everybody ministering
4. Relationships and accountability
5. Single focus

These central values are regularly shared in cell meetings and on Sundays; in the leaflet introducing the church and at the end of each discipleship course for new Christians and members. There is a strong commitment to helping members share their faith and values as a disciple of Christ and members of Harvest, at work and in the wider community.

Places for faith sharing are seen as Alpha courses, social evenings, guest events held in pubs, the Festival of Hope mission in Thanet and On the Move missions. The church grows through new disciples of Christ as much as it does through transfer of membership from other churches.

Luke 10.1-6 (NRSV)

After this the Lord appointed seventy-two others and sent them on ahead of him in pairs to every town and place where he himself intended to go. He said to them, 'The harvest is plentiful, but the labourers are few; therefore ask the Lord of the harvest to send out labourers into his harvest. Go on your way. See I am sending you out like lambs into the midst of wolves. Carry no purse, no bag, no sandals; and greet no one on the road.

Whatever house you enter, first say, "Peace to this house". And if anyone is there who shares in peace, your peace will rest on that person; but if not, it will return to you'.

Suggested activities

- Ideally you will have had a week's notice that in pairs, you will spend five minutes each sharing your personal faith journey. Identify times of deeper awareness of God, worship that has encouraged you, occasions of grace in action and what has been central to your focus as a disciple of Christ.

- Recently a Christian organisation has invited two Muslims to critique and speak into how this Christian mission agency works among Muslims.

- In respect to the un-churched, invite some representatives of the neighbourhood to give you their impression of your church's identity in your community, their understanding of Christianity and what they find helpful. Provide a relaxed small group setting. This requires maturity, confidence and grace.

- Some churches send members out in pairs to intercede and pray for the homes, businesses and communities that God would bless them with peace. It is interesting to note that in some areas when churches initiate a week of prayer, crime rates diminish according to the police. This either suggests all criminals are Christians or intercessory prayer has a place in sharing the love and peace of God in our communities. Consider praying where you shop, commute, when you pass a local school, hospital, town hall, business park or housing estate.

- Use creativity simply and see faith sharing not as giving people the whole message in one go, like a three-course meal. Rather think of access points, related to food, music, sport, interest, age, gender and people groups. Suggest some possibilities.

Questions

- The Bradford Church's Inner Ring Group has in their terms of remit, a commitment to evangelism/evangelisation and inter-faith dialogue, friendship and understanding. What one aspect of the Christian faith would you wish to share with a person from another faith? What question would you like to ask a person from another faith? (Specify which faith when answering.)

- What opportunities are there in your local community to build friendships with people of a different faith, whether Muslim, Hindu, Jewish or Pagan, for example?

- Describe how Christians can share faith with respect, meaning and dignity for the other person? Where does seeking the person of peace in Luke's reading fit into this?

- Luke's Gospel indicates that the labourers are few. How can your church become intentional about sharing faith as part of the normality of discipleship, instead of the exception?

- How is your church seeking to engage with the de-churched that once worshipped with you? Is there a place for reconciliation and learning between the churched and de-churched? How can this be achieved? Recognising past misdemeanours and hurt in these situations is important and therefore, providing a worship space for forgiveness, healing and new beginnings can be a positive step.

- How creative is your church in 'going out' to the un-churched? There are many resources to draw upon to encourage a conversation, for example, using the internet with www.reJesus.co.uk.

- Explore through discovery courses from Alpha www.alpha.org.uk to Essence www.sharejesusinternational.com to More to Life www.vizaviz.org.

- You could use music workshops. One example is a monthly African drumming workshop for children and parents in rural Essex which has over thirty attending. Who has gifts, skills and availability in your church?

- Work out examples of open-ended questions compared to closed questions in dialogue. How should we handle disagreements in terms of different understandings of faith (back to our values again)?

4. Nourishing daily living – 24/7 discipleship and formation

Introduction

The nineteenth and twentieth century were marked by the rise of the debate between religion and science. Religion retreated and a consequence of this was that religious or spiritual faith was relegated to the realm of private discourse and became alienated from discussion in the public realm. This is referred to as the privatisation of faith, a feature that has impacted on Christian life and society's understanding of it.

However, at the same time, the churches have sought to affirm that faith is not limited to private consumerism. Faith is a radical position that impacts the whole person and, therefore, should influence the whole formation of a follower of Christ, as a citizen, neighbour, householder and worker.

What happens in congregational worship is crucial in this respect. Its purpose is not to compartmentalise the worshipper away from life's blessings or harsh realities, but to be a place of encounter with God to hear what God has to say in the present about ethics at work and home, about environmentalism and social justice. There is a sea change afoot that recognises the biblical imperative for disciples to be salt and light in God's world, thus to be agents of transformation and bridge-builders of reconciliation and hope.

For twenty-first-century life, we require spiritual formation and nourishment that equips us for our day-to-day lives. This core value of nourishing daily living is probably the hidden gem of a healthy church. It moves beyond the disciple obediently and faithfully engaging in the daily quiet time of Bible reading and prayer, or of attending the daily Eucharist, to what cell churches and base ecclesial communities have discovered as sharing our lives at a deeper level as God's missionary community.

The story – Northumbria Community

The founders of the Northumbria Community were three people from three church traditions, Anglican, Baptist and Catholic. The Community has grown in numbers from a few and now there are many companions of the Northumbria Community.

The values of the Northumbria Community surround the monastery of the Mother House in Northumbria, Hetton Hall, and the mission of the community. Monastery and mission work in harmony. The monastery has its own mission of nourishing and empowering visitors, equipping those who come for the mission of their workplace and home life. The mission is the dispersed teams of the Northumbria Community who serve across the churches in Britain and Ireland. A galvanising feature of the Community is the publication *Celtic Daily Prayer* which unites companions who are dispersed across the nations. This provides a rich resource of the context of the Community and the roots of Northumbrian spirituality.

The values of the community are its purpose and vision:
- 'a church without walls'
- 'a church on the streets'
- 'a people who demonstrate 'availability and vulnerability'
- 'loose at the edges'
- 'not holding onto what is not ours to keep'.

The Northumbria Community describe themselves not as a replacement for church, but as an expression of church seeking to support the local church. It is a community centred in God that holds three defining questions that are regularly used to evaluate personal and community levels. These are:
1. Whom do you seek?
2. How then shall we live?
3. How shall we sing the Lord's song in a foreign land?

We live at a time when a revision of what we understand church to be is occurring. Some argue that there are only expressions of church and no one case is a full expression, and that if all are partial expressions, we need them all to have a full understanding. The weekly event of Sunday corporate worship is being added to by what is called fresh expressions or emerging church. These pioneering Christian communities occur at times and places reflecting the 24/7 consumer culture in which we now live. These are formed into household churches, cell church, workplace church and networks of church using the internet. In these, the focus is on church as a multi-level reality, a dynamic model rather than a static structure.

Some pictures of the church, such as light or a city on a hill, emphasise the gathered, strongly visible and attractional. While other images of church, like salt and yeast, work by being dispersed, virtually invisible and subversive. There is a need for healthy space for a variety of shapes of being church at least at a pastoral and practical level and in its forms of outreach.

Application

'I'd particularly like the church to own the world of work, pray for it week in week out, talk to people in the congregation who've got jobs about what they do, how they feel about it, what ethical issues they're facing …

People are often very distant from the church, they feel alienated by the institution; they are confused by all the divisions between the denominations. They often don't see the church as a resource for spirituality.' (Industrial Chaplain)

Colossians 3.12–4.1 (NIV)

Therefore, as God's chosen people, holy and dearly loved, clothe yourselves with compassion, kindness, humility, gentleness and patience. Bear with each other and forgive one another if any of you has a grievance against someone. Forgive as the Lord forgave you. And over all these virtues put on love, which binds them all together in perfect unity.

Let the peace of Christ rule in your hearts, since as members of one body you were called to peace. And be thankful. Let the message of Christ dwell among you richly as you teach and admonish one another with all wisdom through psalms, hymns and songs from the Spirit, singing to God with gratitude in your hearts. And whatever you do, whether in word or deed, do it all in the name of the Lord Jesus, giving thanks to God the Father through him.

This passage, from the church leader Paul, is a reminder of the virtues and graces that are hallmarks of Christian spirituality. Reciprocal relationships, in a serving mutuality, that are lived out in conscientious lifestyles.

The bonding agent is that of perfect love, God's love that binds together what was not formally together. We are exhorted that everything we say or do is done in the name of Jesus; in other words, that we bring everything we do to the testing presence of Jesus. We are ambassadors of Christ therefore; we require preparation and training for such a responsibility in all facets of life.

Suggested activities

- Listen to someone's experience as part of a small group that provides nurture and support:

  'I was such a shy mouse – you have no idea! Now I'm still me but I'm able to do things … Part of my confidence has come from the neighbourhood groups because we uphold each other and we are able to share our own hopes and fears as well as those of our neighbours and those we meet every day … I've been enabled by people around here, and by the Holy Spirit.'

- (a) A key factor from this story was the person's openness to grow and mature. Spend some time noting what you value specifically about each person in the group, e.g., their trust, hospitality or that they are down-to-earth. Then have the group facilitator read indiscriminately some comments.

(b)   Private task: on a scale of 1 (weak) to 5 (strong) indicate your desire to grow and mature as a Christian. For what reason have you put that number?

(c)   What would facilitate nourishment in your spiritual life? How could it happen? What might it look like?

(d)   What are the differences and complementary elements of nurturing growth corporately as a congregation and individually?

(e)   How would you design a spiritual growth programme as a local congregation, seeking to address the variety of learning styles and needs? Design a three-month preaching plan – what themes and texts would be crucial to enable a 24/7 spirituality?

- Describe people who inspire you and what characteristics you seek to emulate. They may be Christians from history, artists from music, literature or film, well known or unknown. We all need heroes.

Questions

- What do the Northumbria Community's three questions and the passage from Colossians say to you as a community? Would it be useful to come back to such questions or challenges over time?

- What are the Christian virtues described in the passage from Colossians? How do we live these out in practice? Which ones need more attention, individually and as a Christian community?

- In what forms do you allow other wise Christians to speak into your life, in showing humility and accountability as the people of God?

- We can wear many faces or masks for different contexts, some for sensible reasons, some for hidden purposes. Jesus said *'you will know the truth, and the truth will set you free' (John 8.32)*. Freedom is about being authentic. How authentic are you in the home, workplace, and church, in the neighbourhood and at leisure?

5. Developing shared leadership – empowering teams

LOOK! I DON'T CARE WHAT YOU THINK! WE'RE DEVELOPING SHARED LEADERSHIP!

Introduction

Ellen MacArthur completed her circumnavigation of the globe in the fastest recorded time in March 2005. She accomplished this as the only crew of a seventy-five foot trimaran. Ellen is a pioneering hero of twenty-first-century life. When it seems that most feats and ventures have been achieved on our planet she has re-awakened the quest to discover new challenges against the tyranny of normality and safety in modern western life.

First impressions may suggest this is a story of one woman's success. She originally thought she had a one in five chance of succeeding. On the surface this could affirm the image of the all-singing, all-dancing, and able management guru of a church leader.

Most church analysts would state categorically that the single factor that will determine the fruitfulness and impact of the Christian church is 'leadership, leadership, leadership'. The penetrating question is what kind of leadership?

In TV and radio interviews, Ellen MacArthur insisted on giving due praise and credit to her team who were resident in the UK as they empowered her using satellite communications at the time of her voyage. Thus, her website is called 'Team Ellen' no less! You will find it at www.teamellen.com

It can be the experience of some working people, when they attend congregational worship, that they leave their professional skills outside because they are unwanted in church life. However, when a church takes advantage of the training of its workplace members for the church's mission in the community, the mutual benefits are significant. Church members using their skills serving others, and church leaders empowering others, creates wider community cohesion.

The story – Newfrontiers family of churches

Newfrontiers models the church's ministry in Ephesians chapter 4, with the specific roles of apostles, prophets, pastors, teachers and evangelists. Considerable respect is especially given to the role of apostleship, in terms of seeking godly leaders to emulate, to have as a mentor, or to be trained by. Again, this is sought in the context of relationship. There is a concern to avoid the restrictions of institutional structure. For more information visit www.newfrontiers.xtn.org

While every Newfrontiers church is autonomously governed by local elders, there is the highest respect for and co-operation with the wider Newfrontiers family, expressed, for example, in the network of Ephesians 4 ministry roles [apostles, prophets, evangelists, pastors and teachers]. At the Brighton conference, which is a national gathering of Newfrontiers churches and guest churches, after a conference talk, the Holy Spirit is invited to speak and heal. Apparently, inspired words of prophecy and knowledge concerning the need for specific healing flowed thick and fast. The prophecies were always measured by those on the platform, including Terry Virgo (national leader) and the apostolic team.

Application

From the accompaniment of Newfrontiers, as part of the Building Bridges of Hope learning phase, it was distinguished that a Church leader's style will govern the church's mission focus. Also, where there is mutual confidence between church leaders and lay people and a shared responsibility for vision, leadership and task, there is greater focus on engaging locally in mission by developing the Christian community.

Priority Areas Committee Church of Scotland

Steps have been taken to seek to ensure that the voice of the Priority Areas Churches is heard on the Priority Areas Committee. For example, meetings have taken place in Priority Areas where local people have led worship. The annual consultation has nurtured a sense of shared belonging, and the 'poverty hearings' have taken place at the annual General Assembly [of the Church of Scotland]. But the composition of the Priority Areas Committee together with its word-based methods of working, do not make shared leadership and proper accountability easy. In general, people from the Priority Areas do not attend meetings. Can the Priority Areas Committee develop new ways of listening to the voice of the Priority Areas? What models of leadership can be developed that are appropriate for those in Priority Areas? Questions about forms of leadership are important, and there is a need to affirm those who do not adopt traditional methods.

John 13.2-8 (NRSV)

And during supper Jesus, knowing that the Father had given all things into his hands, and that he had come from God and was going to God, he got up from the table, took off his

outer robe, and tied a towel around himself. Then he poured water into a basin and began to wash the disciples' feet and to wipe them with the towel that was tied around him. He came to Simon Peter, who said him 'Lord, are you going to wash my feet?' Jesus answered, 'You do not know now what I am doing, but later you will understand.' Peter said to him 'You will never wash my feet.' Jesus answered, 'Unless I wash you, you have no share with me.'

Ephesians 4.11-13 (NRSV)

The gifts he gave were that some would be apostles, some prophets, some evangelists, some pastors and teachers, to equip the saints for the work of ministry for building up the body of Christ, until all of us come to the unity of the faith and of the knowledge of the Son of God, to maturity, to the measure of the full stature of Christ.

Questions

- Do you believe in servant leadership? If so, write down some of its demonstrable characteristics in contemporary church life? Discuss your ideas with your neighbour and then discuss the ideas of the whole group.
- The New Testament combines two strands on leadership. There are, first, those who are called and recognised for leadership by those already in authority and given the office of leadership (Titus 1.5). Then, secondly, there are those who have skills and gifts among the congregations who exude leadership (Romans 12.8) who may not have the office of leadership. Both have advantages. Can they be combined and can churches today learn from both styles?
  - (a) How do we as communities of Christ, empower people to use their calling and gifts in the service of God?
  - (b) How can congregations empower those in the office of leadership?
  - (c) How can leaders who hold office enable teams in leadership?
- The Priority Areas Committee recognised the need for different methods to give people in the urban church 'a voice'. Where and how can you listen to the voices of all those among the congregation, in other Christian communities and in the community and wider world?
- What benefit would there be in giving voice to a range of people groups in your situation?
- Ephesians 4 depicts a fivefold ministry: how do those ministries of apostles, prophets, pastors, teachers and evangelists – 'prepare God's people for works of service'? Does your church use different labels but have similar functions? What other ministries might you wish to add – if any?
- What training and development policies do you have locally to nurture new leaders whether younger or older, and for continuing development for existing leaders? How does all that equip for today's challenging mission context?

6. Becoming communities of learning – exploration

Introduction

During 2005, in the British press and on TV, celebrity chef Jamie Oliver mounted a campaign rebelling against turkey twizzlers and chips in school dinners. Oliver was inspired by a school cook from Nottingham, Jeanette Orrey, who was the agent for change in the menu of school dinners in Britain. Her next venture is a training academy for school cooks. Orrey began her quest in 2000, when she was fed up with her cooking role being reduced to opening packets with a pair of scissors. She established a network of farmers and producers to supply her direct with fruit, vegetables, meat and milk. She reintroduced cookery lessons to the school curriculum and even fed the village OAPs in the school dining room. Orrey says 'You can't change things overnight. You've got to keep the children with you. We've taken five years at my school ...' She goes on to say 'Everyone wants school food improved too quickly. We've lost two generations who don't know how to cook'.[2]

The issues faced in changing patterns of behaviour among people are similar whether it is the eating habits of children or the Sunday worship habits of Christians. The well-worn phrase 'we've always done it this way' is no longer adequate as a reason to do church the way we do. Of course, if after reflection and consultation it's found that the way you do church is appropriate for your context and community, then that is appropriate. It's the assumption-based practice that is the problem here. We need to be willing to ask tough questions of ourselves as communities and be willing to learn and to change as a result.

The story – Harvest New Anglican Church, Broadstairs

With the 'everybody growing' and 'everybody ministering' values in Harvest there is an awareness of and commitment to learning at all levels – formally and informally.

---

2. The Guardian, 8 March 2006, G2, pp.10-11.

Formal teaching takes place through Sunday meetings, cells and leaders' days. Many Harvest members share in this teaching and visiting speakers and teams are also invited. Mutual teaching and learning also happens on an informal, though conscious, level through cells (small groups) and general interaction.

Some of the group feel there is a need for more teaching, but some feel there is a need for more learning; that is, putting into practice what has already been taught, in order to reduce the gap between 'what I know' and 'how I live'.

At Harvest the following phrases were given in response to being asked to complete the sentence 'Rabbi, teach us to …'

… live with God as you do

… walk by faith

… listen to you

… know what commitment really means

… use your power

… know how to have an impact.

The answers show that despite having expressed a need for more teaching, most of the group see a greater need to increase the effectiveness of their lives as disciples. The Harvest value of 'everybody ministering' and 'everybody growing' would seem to support this goal.

The discipleship and training programme at Harvest is one of the most important ones in the church. This includes such features as leaders' training events, Bible study, day conferences, the use of teaching notes in cell meetings. Sunday sermons and other informal methods of learning are all evident in Harvest.

Becoming communities of learning can mean the following:

- Moving from a fixed mindset of 'We know-it-all' to 'We have more-to-learn' and, as society changes, realising that so do the challenges of being Christian in the twenty-first century;

- Unlearning old behaviours that are no longer meaningful for today. For instance, exploring different times for corporate worship that accommodate different life styles;

- Using a range of learning methods from audio, to visual and engaging the human senses; for example, labyrinths are becoming popular as a means of spiritual discovery;

- A church that listens and learns in the gospel, and discovers a rhythm of life from hearing, to talking, to discerning leading to action, then reflection and so on.

- There is also a major issue in some churches and traditions where the minister or priest is seen as the expert. The common belief is that they know it all and do not have any more to learn. The congregation is incapable of learning and the minister is unwilling to let others take leadership as they may soon threaten their position and expose their lack of knowledge and skills. That is the challenge to the willingness to be a *community* of learning and to undergo the conversion necessary for this to happen. Such conversion may mean acknowledging vulnerability on the part of the minister and the willingness to take responsibility on the part of the congregation.

Application

Jeremiah 29.1-15 (NIV) – A Letter to the Exiles

This is the text of the letter that the prophet Jeremiah sent from Jerusalem to the surviving elders among the exiles and to the priests, the prophets and all the other people Nebuchadnezzar had carried into exile from Jerusalem to Babylon.

(This was after King Jehoiachin and the queen mother, the court officials and the leaders of Judah and Jerusalem, the craftsmen and the artisans had gone into exile from Jerusalem.) He entrusted the letter to Elasah son of Shaphan and to Gemariah son of Hilkiah, whom Zedekiah king of Judah sent to King Nebuchadnezzar in Babylon. It said:

This is what the LORD Almighty, the God of Israel, says to all those I carried into exile from Jerusalem to Babylon: Build houses and settle down; plant gardens and eat what they produce. Marry and have sons and daughters; find wives for your sons and give your daughters in marriage, so that they too may have sons and daughters. Increase in number there; do not decrease. Also, seek the peace and prosperity of the city to which I have carried you into exile. Pray to the LORD for it, because if it prospers, you too will prosper. Yes, this is what the LORD Almighty, the God of Israel, says: Do not let the prophets and diviners among you deceive you. Do not listen to the dreams you encourage them to have.

They are prophesying lies to you in my name. I have not sent them, declares the LORD. This is what the LORD says: When seventy years are completed for Babylon, I will come to you and fulfil my gracious promise to bring you back to this place. For I know the plans I have for you, declares the LORD, plans to prosper you and not to harm you, plans to give you hope and a future.

Then you will call upon me and come and pray to me, and I will listen to you. You will seek me and find me when you seek me with all your heart. I will be found by you, declares the LORD, and will bring you back from captivity. I will gather you from all the nations and places where I have banished you, declares the LORD, and will bring you back to the place from which I carried you into exile.

This passage is set at the time of the downfall of Judah in 597 BC and the prophet writes to the exiled people, who must have endured a crisis of identity, purpose and hope. They felt lost in a foreign experience and banished from their homeland.

Christian culture watchers today describe the British and Irish church scene as a 'church in exile', unsure of itself and what to make of the society in which it is set. Among a rapidly changing set of values and priorities, there is a shift in power where once there was dominance of influence, to a situation in which the church feels itself to be increasingly rejected, marginalised and misunderstood. Jeremiah's letter in chapter 29 encourages the exiles to learn and then apply this concretely. Thus, first, they are to see and believe that God's purposes are at work in this circumstance, so they are to 'take the long view'. Secondly, they are, as God's people, to engage with life in Babylonia. Thirdly, they are 'to seek the blessing of God' on the Babylonian people.

Suggested activity

Identify three concrete activities that you will pursue to be a learner of Christ, as an individual and as a community of learners of Christ.

Questions

- Harvest's discipleship and formation goal was 'everybody growing' and 'everybody ministering'. Discuss how your best learning occurs, by what means, and how? Is there a connection between learning and doing, that is 'growing and ministering', and do we learn by doing?

- Peter Drucker, leadership and organisational guru, as well as a Christian, wrote 'no longer learning, no longer growing'.[3] Identify what formation and discipleship training has empowered your Christian life. It may have been when you prepared for your first communion, or when you came to Christian faith. Is there a rhythm in learning and growing, like the four seasons? If so what can we learn from each stage?

- Describe how the Israelites would have felt as exiles in a foreign country. What would they miss, what would they feel and how could they have begun the journey of living at home as exiles?

- What similarities are there for the church today with the experience of exile?

- What do we have to let go of and unlearn? What new learning needs to take place? How do we maintain a Christian distinctiveness in a world of pluralism and relativity?

- Consider asking people of different age groups what they make of the church's current services and weekly programme. Why not ask some people who do not attend church their viewpoint of what goes on in your church and what it positively and negatively communicates?

- In the Gospels Jesus does a lot of listening and story-telling over meals. Look up some of these occasions in Luke's gospel. [Luke 7.1-10; 7.36-50; 11.37-41; 14.1-14; 19.5-10; 22.13-30; 24.13-35; 39-49] How can we find creative ways to give time, space and grace to encounter one another? What are your fears or hopes in this possibility?

- Is your church leader enabling others to share in the task of leadership and are your members taking up the challenge of learning to be lay leaders?

---

3. http://jmm.aaa.net.au/ tribute to Peter Drucker who died in 2005.

7. Contributing to and being stimulated by wider networks – enriched by outsiders

AT LEAST
HE'S TRYING
TO NETWORK
AND ADAPT...

GOTH
CHURCH

FAKE
BLOOD

STAGE
MAKE
UP

Introduction

Local congregations can find their denominational structures complex and can feel isolated from them. Within most of the Christian churches are regional staff known as diocesan missioners, mission enablers, regional ministers and so forth, whose task is to assist local congregations with their mission strategy and implementation. In spite of the able and talented officers in these roles, one of the abiding experiences of churches in these times of denominational financial cuts and merging of congregations is the emergence of suspicion that those representing the regional structures report back to the hierarchy unfavourably on local situations.

In contrast, churches that took part in the Building Bridges of Hope mission accompaniment scheme found themselves commenting in surprising ways after entering the process of using a skilful outsider from a different church tradition:

- They discovered encouragement from churches that were not part of their usual tradition or stream. Opposites do attract and can definitely complement!

- They gained fresh perspective through listening to the stories of one another that sparked new possibilities for mission in their context. Being listened to meant that they would consider the creative input of the other.

- Organically developed links with other churches in the Building Bridges of Hope mission accompaniment scheme, including visits and exploration together about what it means to be in God's mission for these times.

The Channel 4 television programme 'Grand Designs' visits households who are embarking on building projects, whether extensions or transformations of existing homes or new house builds in wild and beautiful locations. The programme visits the owners at various stages from start to finish, showing the highs and lows of the building projects. Mission accompaniers fulfil a similar role in providing the outsider's perspective, like the programme presenter who reflects on the homeowners' dreams and plans, comments on their action plan, interpreting experience and asking incisive questions from how to reconfigure a disrupted schedule to fulfil the goals and articulating a summary of the journey and its outcomes.

Mission companions use the primary skills of:

1. Listening
2. Asking incisive questions
3. Reflecting and mirroring
4. Encouraging and supporting
5. Facilitating and interpreting the way forward

The stories

Newfrontiers, as a family of churches across Britain, hold an annual leaders conference each summer. They have fostered excellent relationships with leaders from outside the Newfrontiers family. Many of these have influenced what Newfrontiers do. While they are very clear about the mission that God has called them to, they are open to hear from others in the broader evangelical world.

Some have gone much further and forged links with people beyond their denominational and ecclesial traditions. For instance, Northumbria Community was founded by leaders from the Church of England, Baptist and Roman Catholic churches. The governing body of the Community, the General Chapter, welcomes authorised visitors annually from these traditions to speak into the life of the Community. It's a sign of their submission to God and to the churches they affiliate to.

Accountability and transparency are spiritual disciplines that enable churches, religious communities and cell groups to maintain a healthy balance by allowing the skilled outsider – the mission companion – to affirm, challenge and empower through a committed relationship, which includes connection to a wider network that moves beyond denominational and theological ties.

One of Northumbria Community's principles in living out faith today is 'vulnerability'. To be vulnerable requires security in one's calling from the Lord, and openness to be teachable compared to the attitude of 'know-it-alls'.

The key benefits of appointing a 'mission companion' were recognised by a group of churches in Bradford, with some who had been accompanied remarking that the insights of an outsider enabled them to see themselves in a different light. This is an affirming experience as well as enlightening one. Somebody outside the immediate tradition or church structure may well see such blind spots more clearly – but obviously, they need to be respectful, sensitive and charitable in pointing them out.

Finally, The Bridges Trust in Edenbridge said of accompaniment:

'Accompaniment has helped us to see the way ahead and keep on track.'

It had helped them to consider how overt to be in the Centre with regard to their Christian aims and it has enabled them to be more professional in their approach. As one member commented 'We began to see ourselves as 'church in the community.'

Application

Luke 24.13-35 (NIV) – On the road to Emmaus

Now that same day two of them were going to a village called Emmaus, about seven miles from Jerusalem. They were talking with each other about everything that had happened. As they talked and discussed these things with each other, Jesus himself came up and walked along with them; but they were kept from recognizing him.

He asked them, 'What are you discussing together as you walk along?'

They stood still, their faces downcast. One of them, named Cleopas, asked him, 'Are you only a visitor to Jerusalem and do not know the things that have happened there in these days?'

'What things?' he asked.

'About Jesus of Nazareth,' they replied. 'He was a prophet, powerful in word and deed before God and all the people. The chief priests and our rulers handed him over to be sentenced to death, and they crucified him; but we had hoped that he was the one who was going to redeem Israel. And what is more, it is the third day since all this took place. In addition, some of our women amazed us. They went to the tomb early this morning but didn't find his body. They came and told us that they had seen a vision of angels, who said he was alive. Then some of our companions went to the tomb and found it just as the women had said, but him they did not see.'

He said to them, 'How foolish you are, and how slow of heart to believe all that the prophets have spoken! Did not the Christ have to suffer these things and then enter his glory?' And beginning with Moses and all the Prophets, he explained to them what was said in all the Scriptures concerning himself.

As they approached the village to which they were going, Jesus acted as if he were going farther. But they urged him strongly, 'Stay with us, for it is nearly evening; the day is almost over.' So he went in to stay with them.

When he was at the table with them, he took bread, gave thanks, broke it and began to give it to them. Then their eyes were opened and they recognized him, and he disappeared from their sight. They asked each other, 'Were not our hearts burning within us while he talked with us on the road and opened the Scriptures to us?'

They got up and returned at once to Jerusalem. There they found the Eleven and those with them, assembled together and saying, 'It is true! The Lord has risen and has appeared to Simon.' Then the two told what had happened on the way, and how Jesus was recognized by them when he broke the bread.

In the aftermath of the events of Good Friday, defeat leads two of Jesus' disciples to talk of failure as they leave the city of Jerusalem. The Messiah is dead. On the journey to the village of Emmaus, a stranger, so it seems, starts asking some questions about what's happening. This friendly stranger doesn't tell them who he is and what he can do for them, he teases out what is in their hearts. A relationship bridge is built and they invite the friend to stay for supper. Then the revelation, the fuller understanding occurs and just when they want to possess the risen Christ and become dependent, he disappears and the encounter turns them around heading back into the city of Jerusalem to share with their community the news that the Messiah is risen.

Questions

- Share the disciples' bewilderment, regret and dejection as they walked away from Jerusalem: their friend is dead, their hopes and dreams shattered – 'we had hoped that he was the one who was going to redeem us [Israel]' (verse 21). What hopes and dreams for your church's life and mission have as yet to happen and have left you dejected?

- We take much of what happens in the weekly events of church for granted. Sometimes we can be myopic, interested in the things that only concern us. Jesus asks the simplest of questions about the circumstances of the time – 'what things [have happened]?' (verse 19) What things are happening in your church's activity and mission? How might you show interest and support different aspects of the church's mission?

- In a complex world and a sophisticated church we can forget to remember the simplicity of the Christian faith (verse 25). Imagine you are a stranger to your church and wider community. What would you remind the faith community of?

- The act of breaking of bread (verse 30) was the final disclosure in this journey of discovery. At times we can lose heart to look and discover God in the new as well as ordinary things of life. The disciples return to Jerusalem, to face persecution and misunderstanding, but what's the difference now? What difference do we as a Church need now?

- Read verses 33-35 then tell each other of times when you have recognised the risen Christ with you. Think back over your Christian life and experience. Has anyone ever walked with you like Jesus and helped you see the truth?

The Spirituality of a Bridge-building Church

'The spirituality of a bridge-building Church' may appear an abstract title. However, it is worth giving time to reflect upon since how we practise our Christian faith is at the heart of the kind of community that will be developed. Cement is only good if it has the right quantities of cement mixture, water and the right kind of sand, stirred well.

The added value of mission accompaniment for cultivating, encouraging and supporting a spiritually adventurous attitude in your church is also worth giving thought to. Remember the skilful outsider, the mission companion, can see un-noticed opportunities and strengths you might undervalue and offers the discipline of being transparent as a Christian community. Therefore, what attitudes and thinking are necessary for the environment of a bridge-building church to flourish?

Commitment

Some Christians who work with young people make the observation that young people in the education system are not encouraged to be 'committed' to a position, thought or belief system. Why? It is due to the fact that they are always encouraged to weigh up differing views, as observers, form an opinion, which leads them to become commentators rather than players in life. Given this, it is worth recognising that the basis of Christian commitment is:

1. Commitment to God

God's call to people is a radical biblical call. We know this from the story of Abraham and Sarah who are called not only to believe in a future with offspring despite their age, but sell their bungalow as pensioners to re-locate to a new land! The willingness to uproot and take risks at their age is based on their commitment to God. They take this step of adventure primarily because of God's commitment to them that gives way to hearing God's call for their lives. The danger with this theme is that some Christians who are 'committed' can use it as a club with which to beat the less committed, which hardly invites commitment.

Suggested activities

- In the church's teaching programme consider liaising with the church leadership on a series exploring Abraham or the Minor Prophets call to commitment.
- In prayer gatherings in churches and home groups include prayers of petition, inviting God to search our hearts (Psalm 139.23-24) and praying that we endeavour to model attractive and committed Christian lives.

- Invite newer Christians, however old or young, to step up by assuming a role or task that causes them to trust God, stretch faith and grow their gifts. That means we must not only give room for them, but trust them.

Questions

- What are the signs and evidence of a life committed to God in the Bible?
- In what ways have you grown inwardly and outwardly in commitment to God in recent years?
- Why is commitment such a tough discipline for us all? Consider such themes as yielding, trusting, and availability to God.

2. Commitment to each other

'By this all people will know that you are my disciples.' John 13.35

The crucial ingredient for Christian community is *agape* love. This kind of love is lived out through the life of Jesus and ultimately on the cross. Modern examples include Dietrich Bonhoeffer, Martin Luther King Jr., Oscar Romero and Mother Teresa. The hallmark of a community of disciples is benchmarked by 'self-giving love'.

Once more we see that this is a radical call that pulls largely against the flow of modern society. Christians are called to the new household of God, a new family and to express that new relationship through loving one another. Church can be described as a box of chocolates. We have our favourites, those in the box we find acceptable and those we don't like and leave in the box. And so in our churches the same will apply about the people in it. Nevertheless, the good news is that we are called to love and not called to like – a subtle and important difference. We can all recognise difficulties within Christian communities, history, people and structures. Nevertheless, Jesus Christ has called us to love one another and Jesus measures our obedience to him by the outflow of our commitment to one another (John 15.10-17).

Suggested activities

- In silent prayer allow God to test your love for one another and show you where to develop commitment to one another. Don't look at others around you and compare their quality or lack of commitment – it begins with you. Don't forget that commitment to one another is not an end in itself, but for the purpose of God's mission to the world.
- Express in appropriate ways your thanksgiving: prayer, a message to another who has shown commitment to you.

- What does it means to be 'one in Christ' even though we are all unique and different?
- Which Christians inspire you and why? Think of people in the Bible, Christian history and your local church.

3. Commitment to the de-churched

You might be wondering what the de-churched, as leavers of churches, have to say to you as a bridge-building church. It can be easy to assume we know why people leave our churches. However, it is worth discovering on a case by case basis why people are giving up on Church. As Christians we have a God-given call to be 'bridge-builders' as we remember that the Word became a human being (John 1.14). We follow God, the bridge-builder who came from heaven to earth to reach out to his own Jewish people and subsequently to the entire non-Jewish world.

The ministry of healing and reconciliation has a role to play in drawing alongside the de-churched. However, before this ministry can become effective a healthy attitude by the congregation towards church leavers is vital. We have to ask ourselves whether we really want to have the de-churched back among us. That does mean working through the problems, confession and forgiveness on both sides.

It is a sad situation when congregations have lost the heart to be open Christian communities and to welcome a diverse range of people from different backgrounds.

The account of the Apostle Peter was a marvellous example of an 'over-comer'. When he walked on water and began to sink, Jesus reached out to him. When Peter disowned Jesus and the poignancy of the cock crowing, later we find Jesus rehabilitating Peter – never giving up on who was to become leader of the Jerusalem church. Jesus never gives up on us.

Suggested activities

- Pray (if need be privately) for those church leavers known to you, whether children who have left younger church or adults disillusioned, tempted away or unwanted.
- Consider what strategies of follow up to enquire about the well-being of church leavers can be done. What bridging stations or intermediate, neutral zones could be set up as potential stepping stones back to church for the de-churched?

Questions

- A bridge-building church does a lot of heart searching as to motivation and attitude. What is your attitude to the de-churched? Do they matter to God? Do they matter to your church, if so show how?
- How does the story of the prodigal son inspire you with hope (Luke 15)?

4. Commitment to the non-churched

'If it wasn't for a friend who invited me to his church in the 1980s, at best I would be a nominal believer unconnected to the Church and certainly not an ordained minister of the Church!'

How does your Church's budget reflect commitment to the ministry of outreach to the non-churched? Many churches have exemplary ministries and services to the needs of those outside the church. This is inspiring! In many local churches there is a programme that reaches out to those on the streets and people marginalised with addictions and illnesses. This shows commitment to the un-churched at great cost and service by Christians.

What about our commitment not just to serving people outside the church, but living the life with them? That is, embracing and welcoming the non-churched into Christian community and, moreover, sharing the magnificent story of God's reconciling love in Christ that is personal and cosmic! It seems that we, as Christians, not only face the propaganda that various media circulates about the Christian Church, we also need to overcome our own indifference to sharing the story of the crucified and risen one in sensitive, creative and diverse ways across differing cultures.

Suggested activities

- You could ask a friendly non-Christian to visit the church on a Sunday and at other meetings and appraise the welcome and accessibility of what goes on.
- In small groups ask members to describe what it means for them to be a disciple of Jesus Christ. Why does Christian faith have such a place in their life and what specifically would they like to share with the un-churched about their story?
- Pray for guidance and opportunities in the coming days and weeks.

Questions

- How committed to the non-churched is your church and how committed can it become?
- What simple shorter-term and longer-term plans can be put in place to build a bridge with the non-churched?

Growth

In the UK we enjoy four seasons a year. Each season has significance in purpose and value to us. This is true in our Christian journey as individuals and congregations that go through periods of growth from seedlings to maturity, to the glorious autumn colours and then decay, which eventually leads to renewal.

The term 'growth' may be good news to your church, or in some cases produce fear of failure in others. For a variety of reasons the mainstream churches in the UK have faced an unprecedented decline in the latter half of the twentieth century. But that is not the end of the story and there is no reason to see the Church as defunct. But with all new challenges come the opportunities for re-forming. There are some good news stories from across the spectrum of church traditions that are rediscovering God's vision with renewed purpose and vigour.

Growth does include interior spiritual growth, as well as outward fruitful service using the talents and gifts given to God's people. It does include numerical growth, not only for adults but for children as well. Growth comes through exploring old pathways of Christian spirituality as well as new missiological dimensions. Growth is confidence that we are God's people for this time. With growth comes wisdom, discernment and courage to face the future sure of whose hands we are in. There will be obstacles in the way but we know that these often produce perseverance and determination, which are key attributes for us in these times of possible exile or desert wanderings as Christians in the West.

1. For prayer

Prayer is breath for the follower of Christ. There is a movement of prayer in the UK from the old monastic ways to modern versions known as 'the boiler rooms'. These prayer movements engage in relationships with the borough councillors, MPs, business leaders, educators and churches interceding for them in their roles on a regular and intense basis. Prayer as mission is bridging the false divide of sacred and secular compartments to our lives.

In their primary worship service, usually on Sundays, churches invite members of the congregation to share their vocational lives and prayer needs.

While the regular church prayer meeting does hold a place of esteem, 'disbursed prayer meetings' are also becoming popular. Small groups of people praying in the sixth-form college on a weekly basis. Christian workers praying in the board room at 7 o'clock in the morning, young mothers praying for children and parents in the neighbourhood, the local schools and colleges – are all good examples of disbursed prayer meetings.

Often for church leaders the greatest prayer supporters are the housebound saints who encourage and inspire through their constant prayers and warm support. Prayer is accessible to all, it can be verbal, or non-verbal, liturgical or spontaneous, use articulate language or simple prose, creative art and design, or a collage from daily newspapers to symbolise prayers of intercession or thanksgiving. No matter who you are – or how young or old you are – you are invited to express prayer to God. There is no tax or restriction on praying and we know that God communicates through prayer.

Suggested activities
- Why not organise a prayer walk regularly for your neighbourhood?
- Keep a diary of intercession and look for God's answers: stop, wait or go.

Questions
- What particular concerns has God placed upon your prayer life? Who could you meet up to pray with?
- Discover different types of prayers. What is comfortable or uncomfortable in these differences?
- How can you keep prayer meetings from tiresome familiarity?
- How desperate do you have to be to pray?

2. For worship

One size does not fit all in worship, no matter which theology or tradition of worship your church employs. We live at a time when people appreciate degrees of diversity. Whatever style you prefer, worship needs to be inclusive and take account of the guests as well as linguistically make sense to the uninitiated. In other words, it is important to ask why we do what we do rather than just assert that we do it because we've always done it that way!

Worship is at the centre of congregational life. It is the fulfilling of the first commandment to love God first of all. Worship is more than reciting liturgy, more than singing songs and hymns, more than celebrating the sacraments, more than the exposition of God's word. Worship, biblically, is a 24/7 act – not just on Sunday mornings, but what we do with all of our lives. G. K. Chesterton said 'We say grace before a meal. I say grace before every task and activity.'

What this means is that all activity from corporate worship, our household lives, our leisure and work can be an act of worship in response to God. Therefore, our attitudes can be infused with worship while we cut the lawn or prepare the children for school or gather for a meeting at work. We can offer our time, skills and talent as an act of worship to God.

Suggested activities
- During the coming week as you go about important and routine tasks consciously do it 'as for the Lord'. Monitor your responses.

- Pray with thanksgiving and honesty for the daily activities that they may be an act of worship 'unto the Lord'. Include confession too.
- Observe what subjects are covered in corporate worship and those areas never mentioned in Sunday worship – list them.
- Ask the church leader why there has never been a sermon on 'X' and prayers for 'Y' or Bible reading from 'Z'.

Questions

- How do we divide up our lives between the sacred and secular, those false divides of a higher and lower calling.
- 'Where two or three are gathered there I am in the midst of you', said Jesus (Matthew 18.20). He also said 'Lo I am with you always to the end of the age' (Matthew 28.20) – what's your understanding of the presence of God in life?
- What are signs of a life yielded to God: in the household, workplace, neighbourhood, world, and church?

3. For people not yet in the church

During the Second World War, two Christian leaders bridged a deep divide by prophetic and practical expressions of solidarity. Each day the German pastor Dietrich Bonhoeffer would read the Scriptures in English and George Bell, Bishop of Chichester, read a chapter of the Bible in the German language.

What signs of solidarity can we as Christians show to those outside the church? What action against evil can we take to reveal that we are on the side of the God of justice?

The saying 'you've got to walk the talk' is true in order to earn the right to be heard.

Intentionality is a key ingredient. There will be resistance to church growth. With growth comes change. As a church do we wish to be intentional about reaching the lost, practising the ministry of listening and healing to the bruised and being difference makers in society? It is as basic as that. Or has church become a private members' club?

God so loved the world: you, your neighbours, the sinned against, and perpetrators of evil. It doesn't have to be complicated since it can begin a person at a time. If God so loves the world, the sending God beckons us to be intentional in bridging the gap as ambassadors of his love and call to *metanoia*, which means 'turning around to Christ'.

Suggested activities

- In your small group explore what particularly captivates you about Jesus Christ and God.

- If your church has a vision or mission statement, look for the intention to reach out to people as yet not in the church. How is this being worked out? This is not a clean process, mission is messy!
- As a group write your own statement of values to grow and include those outside the church

Questions
- Where is the biblical mandate to reach out to those not yet part of the church?
- Imagine a non-church person asked you this question, how would you answer it? 'Why should I join the church, what's in it for me?'

Change

Tradition is good and most of us tend not to want our traditions to change. However, when tradition becomes traditionalism it is wrong. It can then become rigid and unthinking and we can end up worshipping our past, rather than seeking also to respond to the present and all that is good in it too. Change is normal and always around us but we often seek to keep the church institution exactly the same.

Some changes are good. Many people yearn for the change of their summer or winter vacation! Maybe we need to take a view that in some churches the way we do church requires a vacation, a period to experiment and explore.

The seasons remind us that life is a journey of change. Therefore, the challenge for us as believers is to live with our hands lightly on the steering wheel of life, permitting positive change and adjusting to times of unwelcome change. A person's mental health is linked to the capacity to adapt and be flexible through life. This is true for the church as well.

A 'multiple approach' for church life is one way forward. For instance, some churches experiment with several morning services to meet different needs.

Change requires confidence and security in who we are called to be as the people of God. It requires focus on the motives and intentions of why we are here and where we are going. With these in place and reasons understood, change becomes less fearful.

Suggested activities

It's unsurprising we are negative toward change since the cost of change in our world has been born at a high price ecologically and on many other levels.
- Do some research among different age groups to ask what they like about new people entering our churches and why they don't like new people joining our churches. People need to be anonymous and names kept confidential.

- Get your small group to either purchase or borrow the book *The Road Less Travelled* by M. Scott Peck and agree a reading and reflection plan over four weeks using the chapter headings.
- During a month, keep a record of areas of change that bring frustration and joy, at home, work, church, nationally and globally.

Questions

- How open to change is your church: resistant, moderate or willing? It may well depend on what is up for change, so identify the hot potato issues?
- How can an open attitude to reasonable change be cultivated in churches?
- What one thing would you like to change about your church and yourself?

Contextualisation

In the climate of church planting, fresh expressions of church and emerging church, more than ever the realisation is that the key to mission is that the church must relate to its own cultural context. Mission accompaniment can facilitate this translation process between church and culture.

Community researchers ('culture watchers') provide helpful information for churches in perceiving and understanding the mores and values around us (paradigms – world views). International mission training has shown that observing and listening to culture is vital in order to have an impact and be transformative in a different culture. The role of mission accompaniment will offer guidance on how to research your context as well as interpret opportunities presented that can be strategically planned.

Suggested activities

- Invite a number of un-churched friends and interview them together on given subjects of concern in your community to understand how to relate your church's call to mission to local issues.
- During the next week, take newspaper cuttings or webnews headlines and discuss the underlying values and connecting points for the church's mission engagement.

Questions

- Read Romans 12.1-3. How have your thinking and attitudes been transformed by God in the last five years?
- What concerns might you have about over or under-contextualising as a church? In other words how does your church relate to your local community? Does your church understand itself as standing within the local community or separate from it?

Can you see the value of mission accompaniment and has your church appointed a mission companion?

Reproductive churches

Christian missioners speak of the biblical principle of reproducing ministries meaning that the DNA of the church is life giving. By this we mean that we look to share what we have been given by God with other inherited and emerging Christian communities – we look beyond the end point of service alone, instead, recognising that God calls us to be reproductive churches. A good example would be the Alpha Course experience, that one church runs an Alpha course and then facilitates another to be started in a neighbouring town.

1. Reproduction of ministries

One of the Building Bridges of Hope actions pilots, DNA Networks, Colchester has an in-built philosophy that it does not tell people what to do in the use of their gifts, but rather invites believers to get involved with what stirs their hearts. This means involvement in the areas of ministry they are passionate about. What would your church look like if people did what they are inspired to do?

If your church has a specialist ministry expertise, say, cross-cultural service, how could you share the insights you've gained and so spark new ministries in other churches in similar contexts?

2. Reproduction of churches

The Acts of the Apostles is the dynamic account of the birthing of new Christian communities. With the decline and closure of some historic churches and emergence of new housing estates – we live in a time where establishing Christian communities are once again a priority. For some, it will be commencing new churches, not buildings, but churches that meet in the community centre or school. This is not about competing with existing churches, but reaching the 92.5% of people not part of the Christian church in any tangible way!

3. Reproduction of mission accompaniment

Time will reveal how the biblical concept of being accompanied on our journey to growth develops. Are there people in your church who might exercise this ministry to others, receive training and serve other Churches in this way? In John's Gospel chapter 14 'the Paraclete', the Holy Spirit, we are told by Jesus will come alongside to encourage us. The word 'para' means literally 'alongside'. Mission companions are fortifiers. They are Christians who are primarily there to encourage and strengthen the mission of the church.

4. Reproduction of Christian love

If the language of 'reproduction' still doesn't make sense as a biblical principle, then it may be more helpful to some to use the biblical language about reproducing

Christian love. Thus, we aim at being and producing intentional places of divine presence and acceptance. A church in London was developed on the biblical foundation of grace. What an exciting theology in which to birth a Christian community – that God's everlasting, surefooted, steadfast and constant love would be the rule of this emerging community! People from whatever background or situation would be welcomed. That didn't mean there was no accountability but rather the primary driver was to be a God shaped community, modelled on Jesus. So often our churches model other churches, traditions, or organisations.

Christian love is the defining feature that we are told we take with us into the Kingdom of Heaven. How are we encouraging new believers to invest in the love of Christ?

Suggested activities

- Maybe the theme of reproductive churches is new or a different way of seeing the church's purpose. If the church were an apple tree should it produce apples or in fact more apple trees? Discuss!
- Do you know the history of your local church – who started it, when and at what sacrifice? Who started the various ministry areas of the church? Note what has become obsolete and what continues today.

Questions

- In families we often see a likeness in habits and characters through the generations perpetuated. What would you like to see multiplied (reproduced) in your church for the next generations?
- In your small group draw up a mission plan of how you could multiply the four areas above, ministries, churches, mission accompaniment and love? How and when can this happen?

The Accompanied Mission Journey

The skills of a mission companion

By this stage you may well have completed your own study and reflection of the seven core values. Hopefully, it will have encouraged you to consider afresh what God is calling you to as a local congregation or project.

If you have not deployed the services of a mission companion, we would strongly recommend you do, in order to attain the aims and goals that have emerged.

Listening: That is, active listening. This means that instead of thinking what you are going to say concentration is focused on how and what is being said, or not said. Is what is being said relevant to the purpose? Transparency can be assisted by tone of voice and posture.

Questions: That are incisive about what it means to be in God's will today? How a group understands the needs and hopes of a church?

Discussion: To provide clarity of purpose, thought and cohesion.

Reflection: That offers an impartial viewpoint and constructive analysis.

Interpretation: Holding the big picture whilst managing the details.

Facilitation: Enabling voices to be heard and a coherent perspective to the situation.

Signposting: The availability of numerous resources for churches to use in specific contexts. For example, tools for community audits, or congregational audits; developing initiatives and skills for mission engagement with particular people groups from young people to ethnic minority groups.

How does Mission Accompaniment work in practice?

- *Consultation:* This needs to happen in the local congregation to agree to the purpose of appointing a mission accompanier and also to identify areas for the accompaniment to address.

- *The terms of agreement:* This follows on from the consultation in the local church in that it will identify three of the 'seven core values of a mission church'. The formation of a co-ordination group or reference group that the mission companion will meet with.

- *Selection of a mission accompanier:* The Centre for Mission Accompaniment can give advice on this part of the process. Contact the address at the end of this publication.

- *Accompaniment underway:* The mission companion would initially wish to spend one or two sessions 'getting to know' the local church by attending certain prescribed meetings, for example, a PCC or deacons' meeting, or various weekly events of the church.

What are the benefits and challenges?

The Building Bridges of Hope scheme has built a strong reputation for matching mission companions to churches and projects. The majority have been in local churches, but some are at regional and national denominational level. One of the key principles in the Building Bridges of Hope scheme is that mission companions were chosen from one Christian tradition and then matched to another Christian tradition. Churches were matched from different theological and liturgical traditions. For example, an evangelical Anglican alongside a Roman Catholic Church worked very well. It was important to look for synergy and empathy between the match of local church and mission accompanier in particular in understanding the mission of God. Above all, the overall guiding principle has been that the local church makes the decisions!

At first, to some churches the thought of a mission companion arriving from a different Christian tradition might appear a distraction. Some could argue that someone is needed who understands how our church tradition ticks, rather than waste time explaining the niceties of denominational governance. The experience in the Building Bridges of Hope scheme has been the opposite. The mission companion who comes from outside the host tradition brings the following benefits.

- *Impartiality:* The mission companion comes with 'no strings attached'. Their desire is to encourage the host church to develop their engagement in God's mission. They have no ties to the host's denominational hierarchy, so there need be no fears of reporting back to the powers that be. This is crucial in developing trust.

- *Mutual learning:* The mission companion will learn and develop as much as the host church has to benefit. In today's paradigm many church adherents no longer affiliate because of denominational doctrines, but rather look for church style and provision of certain ministries.

- *Long-term, sustained accompaniment:* Once a mission companion is appointed, their visits will range between monthly to quarterly, depending on the terms of agreement. The duration of these ranges from 18 months to 3 years. In church life a number of unexpected occurrences can deflect our attention, whether a crisis within the congregation, or building project that is delayed or a change of leadership. The mission companion together with a co-ordinating team (reference group whom the mission companion principally meets with) can seek to keep hold of the focus and encourage the church when it's tough going.

- *Skilful methodology:* The mission companion is a Christian with experience from their local church, who comes recommended with their own skills and experiences. The seven core values of a mission church provide the lens through which to focus the visits during the accompaniment. We suggest the host church determines the top three core values that relate to their needs to begin the first year of accompaniment.

- *Sustainable church development:* Mission accompaniment is a supportive, focused and empowering process to integrate creative change throughout the church's life. Seeking to integrate a holistic programme of points of engagement, reaching parts other fail to touch!

Mission accompaniment is a process, a journey of discovery to learn and affirm God's unique calling to your church that will differ to others.

What of the challenges and opportunities?

- *Openness and transparency:* The rapport and trust that develops between a mission companion and church is crucial for a creative relationship, where revealing unanswered questions, areas of perceived weakness as well as strengths is crucial. Particularly, those who hold influence among our churches need a maturity to allow the outsider to speak thoughtfully into the life of the church.

- *Providing space for all:* For mission accompaniment to be of value, the whole congregation at some level needs to be part of the input and output of the next steps. The process of listening and asking questions demands an accountability to take these seriously and not sweep issues under the carpet. Therefore, access points for the congregation to learn of what is happening during the course of accompaniment is essential.

- *Authority:* A co-ordination team (reference group whom the mission companion principally interacts) is established that is not only made up of elected officers/leaders, but different representatives of the congregation, age, gender and emphasis. The co-ordination team needs teeth to make decisions. Also, timelines for goals need calculating in the contracting of the accompaniment process.

Ultimately, the more open you are to the accompaniment experience the greater the benefit.

I'M AFRAID IT'S AN OCCUPATIONAL HAZARD...

How can we find a mission companion?

The options before you are either

1. Contact the Centre for Mission Accompaniment either by phone, email or visit the website to obtain advice on finding a mission companion.

   or

2. Self-select your own mission accompanier, perhaps someone you know who has a good reputation.

The process of selecting a mission accompanier, known as the 'matching process' has the following steps:

- *The terms of agreement:* The expected areas of church life to be accompanied, hoped for outcomes, the seven core values.
- *Selection of a mission companion:* Church tradition, skills and experience sought, the duration and frequency of visits by the mission companion.
- *Establish a co-ordination team (reference group):* This includes members involved from the officers of the church leadership (minister/priest, deacons, PCC or Elders) as well as various people from the congregation adding strength and depth to the team.
- *Initiating the process of accompaniment:* The mission companion will listen to the church's story, visiting various church and community meetings, including a Sunday service.
- *Review and assessment reports:* Periodic evaluation between mission companion and the co-ordination team to re-negotiate boundaries, sharpen focus, change the duration of accompaniment and areas addressed.
- *The end of accompaniment:* Celebrate the learning and development; acknowledge areas that need further attention and strategies to ensure implementation after the accompanied journey.

The cost of deploying a mission accompanier

The benefits of recruiting a mission companion are evident from earlier phases of work in Building Bridges of Hope. The general cost for the work of a mission companion over a period of a year is approximately £500.

However, this can be negotiated up or down depending on the size and context of the church requesting a mission companion and the circumstances of the mission companion.

Appendix

The Evolution of Mission Accompaniment and the Building Bridges of Hope Project

It was during an international conference in the mid 1990s in Potsdam, Germany that British and Irish church leaders and representatives listened to Lesslie Newbigin speak of the imperative of the local church as a missionary congregation. At the same gathering an animated story was told by Gerhard Linn of how the former East German church sought to be missionary in a restrictive environment, which brought about the birth of the accompanied missionary congregation model. It was these stories that ignited the imagination of British and Irish church leaders to initiate the 'Building Bridges of Hope' mission accompaniment project from Churches Together in Britain and Ireland (CTBI).

Phase A (1995-1996) was the agreement from the mission and evangelism departments across the churches of the Four Nations with some missionary agencies to sponsor, advise and define the scope of work.

Phase B (1996-2000) involved forty local churches from Catholic to Pentecostal traditions across the UK and Ireland receiving a quarterly visit during three years by a skilful outsider termed the 'participant observer'. This research explored how churches engaged, educated, evangelised and equipped congregations. The fruit of this research is now called 'the seven core values of a mission church'. These are characteristics of a church that is seeking to honour and respond to the calling into God's mission. The publication of this report 'God's Mission in the local church' is free to download at www.ctbi.org.uk (section: downloads).

Phase C (2001-2006) was a piece of action research on the seven core values of a mission church. Thirty-five churches across Britain and Ireland were accompanied by a mission companion from a different church / tradition. What was crucial in this work was the significant effect of the mission companion and the skills, methods, rapport and duration of accompaniment.

The final piece of the jigsaw and harvest of the decade of Building Bridges of Hope is the formation of the Centre for Mission Accompaniment, organised by the Global Mission Network of CTBI. The Centre's focus will be the promotion of mission accompaniment as a means in realigning churches in the pursuit of God's mission using mission companions. It hopes to provide training for mission companions and resources for churches, both in their local expressions and in other forms and levels of church, and to build partnerships in this discipline with both inherited and emerging churches in England, Wales, Scotland and Ireland.